This book belongs to:

<u>miss K Krepps</u>
I will miss you over the
years. Thanks for helping me

PSALMS
for
TODAY

INSPIRATIONAL KEEPSAKES
FROM LONGMEADOW PRESS:

Proverbs for Today

Psalms for Today

Reflections from Jesus

Passages for Consolation

PSALMS
for
TODAY

Edited by Michael Myers

LONGMEADOW PRESS

Jacket design by Lisa Amoroso
Interior design by Lisa Amoroso
ISBN: 0-681-41443-X
Printed in U.S.A.
First Edition
0 9 8 7 6 5 4 3 2 1

Blessed *is* the man that walketh not in the counsel of the ungodly, nor standeth in the way of sinners, nor sitteth in the seat of the scornful.

But his delight *is* in the law of the LORD; and in his law doth he meditate day and night.

And he shall be like a tree planted by the rivers of water, that bringeth forth his fruit in his season; his leaf also shall not wither, and whatsoever he doeth shall prosper.

Psalm 1:1–3

The words of the LORD *are* pure words: *as* silver tried in a furnace of earth, purified seven times.

Thou shalt keep them, O LORD, thou shalt preserve them from this generation for ever.

Psalm 12:6, 7

The fool hath said in his heart, *There is* no God.

Psalm 14:1

The LORD also will be a refuge for the oppressed, a refuge in times of trouble

Psalm 9:9

The heavens declare the glory of God; and the firmament sheweth his handywork.

Day unto day uttereth speech, and night unto night sheweth knowledge.

There is no speech nor language, *where* their voice is not heard.

Psalm 19:1–3

The law of the LORD *is* perfect, converting the soul: the testimony of the LORD *is* sure, making wise the simple.

The statutes of the LORD *are* right, rejoicing the heart: the commandment of the LORD *is* pure, enlightening the eyes.

The fear of the LORD *is* clean, enduring for ever: the judgments of the LORD *are* true *and* righteous altogether.

More to be desired *are they* than gold, yea, than much fine gold: sweeter also than honey and the honeycomb.

Moreover by them is thy servant warned: and in keeping of them *there is* great reward.

Psalms 19:7–11

Who shall ascend into the hill of the LORD? or who shall stand in his holy place?

He that hath clean hands, and a pure heart; who hath not lifted up his soul unto vanity, nor sworn deceitfully.

Psalm 24:3, 4

Let integrity and uprightness preserve me; for I wait on thee.

Psalm 25:21

Remember not the sins of my youth, nor my transgressions: according to thy mercy remember thou me for thy goodness sake, O LORD.

Psalm 25:7

For his anger *endureth but* a moment; in his favour *is* life: weeping may endure for a night, but joy *cometh* in the morning.

Psalm 30:5

The LORD *is* my shepherd; I shall not want.

He maketh me to lie down in green pastures: he leadeth me beside the still waters.

He restoreth my soul: he leadeth me in the paths of righteousness for his name's sake.

Yea, though I walk through the valley of the shadow of death, I will fear no evil: for thou *art* with me; thy rod and thy staff they comfort me.

Thou preparest a table before me in the presence of mine enemies: thou anointest my head with oil; my cup runneth over.

Surely goodness and mercy shall follow me all the days of my life: and I will dwell in the house of the LORD for ever.

Psalm 23

O taste and see that the LORD *is* good: blessed *is* the man *that* trusteth in him.

Psalm 34:8

Fret not thyself because of evildoers, neither be thou envious against the workers of iniquity.

For they shall soon be cut down like the grass, and wither as the green herb.

Trust in the LORD, and do good; *so* shalt thou dwell in the land, and verily thou shalt be fed.

Psalm 37:1–3

Be ye not as the horse, *or* as the mule, *which* have no understanding: whose mouth must be held in with bit and bridle, lest they come near unto thee.

Psalm 32:9

Thou lovest righteousness, and hatest wickedness: therefore God, thy God, hath anointed thee with the oil of gladness above thy fellows.

Psalm 45:7

The counsel of the LORD standeth for ever, the thoughts of his heart to all generations.

Psalm 33:11

What man *is he that* desireth life, *and* loveth *many* days, that he may see good?

Keep thy tongue from evil, and thy lips from speaking guile.

Depart from evil, and do good; seek peace, and pursue it.

Psalm 34:12–14

The steps of a *good* man are ordered by the LORD: and he delighteth in his way.

Though he fall, he shall not be utterly cast down: for the LORD upholdeth *him with* his hand.

I have been young, and *now* am old; yet have I not seen the righteous forsaken, nor his seed begging bread.

Psalm 37:23–25

A little that a righteous man hath *is* better than the riches of many wicked.

Psalm 37:16

I delight to do thy will, O my God: yea, thy law *is* within my heart.

Psalm 40:8

Come, behold the works of the LORD, what desolations he hath made in the earth.

He maketh wars to cease unto the end of the earth; he breaketh the bow, and cutteth the spear in sunder; he burneth the chariot in the fire.

Psalm 46:8, 9

Fearfulness and trembling are come upon me, and horror hath overwhelmed me.

And I said, Oh that I had wings like a dove! *for then* would I fly away, and be at rest.

Psalm 55: 5, 6

In God have I put my trust: I will not be afraid what man can do unto me.

Psalm 56:11

Some *trust* in chariots, and some in horses: but we will remember the name of the LORD our God.

Psalm 20:7

They that trust in their wealth, and boast themselves in the multitude of their riches;

None *of them* can by any means redeem his brother, nor give to God a ransom for him:

Psalm 49:6, 7

Cast thy burden upon the LORD, and he shall sustain thee: he shall never suffer the righteous to be moved.

Psalm 55:22

The sacrifices of God *are* a broken spirit: a broken and a contrite heart, O God, thou will not despise.

Psalm 51:17

The fool hath said in his heart, *There is* no God.

Psalm 53:1

O God, thou hast taught me from my youth: and hiterto have I declared thy wondrous works.

Now also when I am old and greyheaded, O God, forsake me not; until I have shewed thy strength unto *this* generation, *and* thy power to every one *that* is to come.

Psalm 71: 17, 18

Give ear, O my people, *to* my law: incline your ears to the words of my mouth.

We will not hide *them* from their children, shewing to the generation to come the praises of the LORD, and his strength, and his wonderful works that he hath done.

That the generation to come might know *them,* *even* the children *which* should be born; *who* should arise and declare *them* to their children:

That they might set their hope in God, and not forget the works of God, but keep his commandments.

Psalm 78: 1, 4, 6, 7

Praise ye the LORD. Praise God in his sanctuary: praise him in the firmament of his power.

Praise him for his mighty acts: praise him according to his excellent greatness.

Praise him with the sound of the trumpet: praise him with the psaltery and harp.

Praise him with the timbrel and dance: praise him with stringed instruments and organs.

Praise him upon the loud cymbals: praise him upon the high sounding cymbals.

Psalm 150: 1–5

Be of good courage, and he shall strengthen
your heart, all ye that hope in the LORD.

Psalm 31:24

Put not your trust in princes, *nor* in the son of
man, in whom *there is* no help.

His breath goeth forth, he returneth to his earth;
in that very day his thoughts perish.

Psalm 146:3, 4

Lo, children *are* an heritage of the LORD: and the fruit of the womb *is his* reward.

As arrows *are* in the hand of a mighty man; so *are* children of the youth.

Happy *is* the man that hath his quiver full of them.

Psalm 127:3–5

I made haste, and delayed not to keep thy commandments.

Psalm 119:60

It is a good thing to give thanks unto the LORD, and to sing praises unto thy name, O most High:

To shew forth thy lovingkindness in the morning, and thy faithfulness every night,

O LORD, how great are thy works! *and* thy thoughts are very deep.

A brutish man knoweth not; neither doth a fool understand this.

Psalm 92: 1, 2, 5, 6

The LORD *is* merciful and gracious, slow to anger, and plenteous in mercy.

He will not always chide: neither will he keep *his anger* for ever.

He hath not dealt with us after our sins; nor rewarded us according to our iniquities.

Psalm 103:8–10

Thy word *is* a lamp unto my feet, and a light unto my path.

Psalm 119:105

Light is sown for the righteous, and gladness for the upright in heart.

Psalm 97:11

The works of his hands *are* verity and judgment; all his commandments *are* sure.

They stand fast for ever and ever, *and* are done in truth and uprightness.

Psalm 111:7, 8

He shall judge the poor of the people, he shall save the children of the needy, and shall break in pieces the oppressor.

Psalm 72:4

Great peace have they which love thy law.

Psalm 119:165

Mercy and truth are met together; righteousness and peace have kissed *each other*.

Psalm 85:10

Give us help from trouble: for vain *is* the help of man.

Psalm 60:11

The LORD *is* on my side; I will not fear: what can man do unto me?

It is better to trust in the LORD than to put confidence in man.

It is better to trust in the LORD than to put confidence in princes.

Psalm 118: 6, 8, 9

It is good for me that I have been afflicted; that I might learn thy statutes.

Psalm 119:71

Let the righteous smite me; *it shall be* a kindness: and let him reprove me; *it shall be* an excellent oil.

Psalm 141:5

Blessed *are* they that keep his testimonies, *and that* seek him with the whole heart.

Psalm 119:2

LORD, thou hast been our dwelling place in all generations.

Before the mountains were brought forth, or ever thou hadst formed the earth and the world, even from everlasting to everlasting, thou *art* God.

For a thousand years in thy sight *are but* as yesterday when it is past, and *as* a watch in the night.

The days of our years *are* threescore years and ten; and if by reason of strength *they be* fourscore years, yet *is* their strength labour and sorrow; for it is soon cut off, and we fly away.

So teach *us* to number our days, that we may apply *our* hearts unto wisdom.

Psalm 90:1, 2, 4, 10, 12

Behold, how good and how pleasant *it is* for brethren to dwell together in unity!

Psalm 133:1

The LORD upholdeth all that fall, and raiseth up all *those that be* bowed down.

Psalm 145:14

Let every thing that hath breath praise the LORD. Praise ye the LORD.

Psalm 150:6

He that dwelleth in the secret place of the most High shall abide under the shadow of the Almighty.

Thou shalt not be afraid for the terror by night, *nor* for the arrow *that* flieth by day;

A thousand shall fall at thy side, and ten thousand at thy right hand; *but* it shall not come nigh thee.

There shall no evil befall thee, neither shall any plague come nigh thy dwelling.

For he shall give his angels charge over thee, to keep thee in all thy ways.

He shall call upon me, and I will answer him: I *will be* with him in trouble; I will deliver him, and honour him.

Psalm 91:1, 5, 7, 10, 11, 15

Lord, thou hast heard the desire of the humble: thou wilt prepare their heart, thou wilt cause thine ear to hear:

To judge the fatherless and the oppressed, that the man of the earth may no more oppress.

Psalm 10:17, 18

The Lord shall cut off all flattering lips, *and* the tongue that speaketh proud things:

Psalm 12:3

LORD, who shall abide in thy tabernacle? who shall dwell in thy holy hill?

He that walketh uprightly, and worketh righteousness, and speaketh the truth in his heart.

He that backbiteth not with his tongue, nor doeth evil to his neighbour, nor taketh up a reproach against his neighbour.

Psalm 15:1–3

The eyes of all wait upon thee; and thou givest them their meat in due season.

Thou openest thine hand, and satisfiest the desire of every living thing.

Psalm 145:15, 16

The lines are fallen unto me in pleasant *places;* yea, I have a goodly heritage.

I will bless the L ORD, who hath given me counsel: my reins also instruct me in the night seasons.

I have set the L ORD always before me: because *he is* at my right hand, I shall not be moved.

Therefore my heart is glad, and my glory rejoiceth: my flesh also shall rest in hope.

For thou wilt not leave my soul in hell; neither wilt thou suffer thine Holy One to see corruption.

Thou wilt shew me the path of life: in thy presence *is* fulness of joy; at thy right hand *there are* pleasures for evermore.

Psalm 16:6–11

I Will love thee, O Lord, my strength.

The Lord *is* my rock, and my fortress, and my deliverer; my God, my strength, in whom I will trust; my buckler, and the horn of my salvation, *and* my high tower.

I will call upon the Lord, *who is worthy* to be praised.

Psalm 18:1–3

Search me, O God, and know my heart: try me, and know my thoughts:

And see if *there be any* wicked way in me, and lead me in the way everlasting.

Psalm 139:23, 24

With the merciful thou wilt shew thyself merciful; with an upright man thou wilt shew thyself upright;

For thou wilt save the afflicted people; but wilt bring down high looks.

For thou wilt light my candle; the LORD my God will enlighten my darkness.

For by thee I have run through a troop; and by my God have I leaped over a wall.

Psalm 18:25, 27–29

O send out thy light and thy truth: let them lead me.

Psalm 43:3

Thou hast also given me the shield of thy salvation: and thy right hand hath holden me up, and thy gentleness hath made me great.

Thou hast enlarged my steps under me, that my feet did not slip.

Psalm 18:35, 36

Judge me, O LORD; for I have walked in mine integrity: I have trusted also in the LORD; *therefore* I shall not slide.

Examine me, O LORD, and prove me; try my reins and my heart.

For thy lovingkindness *is* before mine eyes: and I have walked in thy truth.

I have not sat with vain persons, neither will I go in with dissemblers.

I have hated the congregation of evil doers; and will not sit with the wicked.

Psalm 26:1–5

One *thing* have I desired of the LORD, that will I seek after; that I may dwell in the house of the LORD all the days of my life, to behold the beauty of the LORD, and to inquire in his temple.

Psalm 27:4

He healeth the broken in heart, and bindeth up their wounds.

He telleth the number of the stars; he calleth them all by *their* names.

Great *is* our Lord, and of great power: his understanding *is* infinite.

The LORD lifteth up the meek: he casteth the wicked down to the ground.

Psalm 147:3–6

Hide not thy face *far* from me; put not thy servant away in anger: thou hast been my help; leave me not, neither forsake me, O God of my salvation.

When my father and my mother forsake me, then the LORD will take me up.

Teach me thy way, O LORD, and lead me in a plain path, because of mine enemies.

Psalm 27:9–11

The angel of the LORD encampeth round about them that fear him, and delivereth them.

Psalm 34:7

For the word of the LORD *is* right; and all his works *are done* in truth.

He loveth righteousness and judgment: the earth is full of the goodness of the LORD.

By the word of the LORD were the heavens made; and all the host of them by the breath of his mouth.

He gathereth the waters of the sea together as an heap: he layeth up the depth in storehouses.

For he spake, and it was *done;* he commanded, and it stood fast.

Psalm 33:4–7, 9

Delight thyself also in the LORD; and he shall give thee the desires of thine heart.

Commit thy way unto the LORD; trust also in him; and he shall bring *it* to pass.

Rest in the LORD, and wait patiently for him: fret not thyself because of him who prospereth in his way, because of the man who bringeth wicked devices to pass.

For evildoers shall be cut off: but those that wait upon the LORD, they shall inherit the earth.

For yet a little while, and the wicked *shall* not *be*; yea, thou shalt diligently consider his place, and it *shall* not *be*.

But the meek shall inherit the earth; and shall delight themselves in the abundance of peace.

Psalm 37:4, 5, 7, 9–11

Wait on the LORD, and keep his way, and he shall exalt thee to inherit the land: when the wicked are cut off, thou shalt see *it*.

I have seen the wicked in great power, and spreading himself like a green bay tree.

Yet he passed away, and, lo, he *was* not: yea, I sought him, but he could not be found.

Mark the perfect *man*, and behold the upright: for the end of *that* man *is* peace.

Psalm 37:34–37

God *is* our refuge and strength, a very present help in trouble.

Therefore will not we fear, though the earth be removed, and though the mountains be carried into the midst of the sea;

Though the waters thereof roar *and* be troubled, *though* the mountains shake with the swelling thereof.

Psalm 46:1–3

Have mercy upon me, O God, according to thy lovingkindness: according unto the multitude of thy tender mercies blot out my transgressions.

Wash me throughly from mine iniquity, and cleanse me from my sin.

For I acknowledge my transgressions and my sin *is* ever before me.

Psalm 51:1–3

For a day in thy courts *is* better than a thousand. I had rather be a doorkeeper in the house of my God, than to dwell in the tents of wickedness.

For the LORD God *is* a sun and shield: the LORD will give grace and glory: no good *thing* will he withhold from them that walk uprightly.

Psalm 84:10, 11

In the day of my trouble I will call upon thee: for thou wilt answer me.

Psalm 86:7

Teach me thy way, O LORD; I will walk in thy truth: unite my heart to fear thy name.

Psalm 86:11

The heavens *are* thine, the earth also *is* thine: *as for* the world and the fulness thereof, thou hast founded them.

Justice and judgment *are* the habitation of thy throne: mercy and truth shall go before thy face.

Blessed *is* the people that know the joyful sound: they shall walk, O LORD, in the light of thy countenance.

Psalm 89:11, 14, 15

LORD, how long shall the wicked, how long shall the wicked triumph?

They slay the widow and the stranger, and murder the fatherless.

Yet they say, The LORD shall not see, neither shall the God of Jacob regard *it*.

Understand, ye brutish among the people: and *ye* fools, when will ye be wise?

He that planted the ear, shall he not hear? he that formed the eye, shall he not see?

Psalm 94:3, 6–9

The LORD knoweth the thoughts of man, that they *are* vanity.

Psalm 94:11

Unless the LORD *had been* my help, my soul had almost dwelt in silence.

And he shall bring upon them their own iniquity, and shall cut them off in their own wickedness; *yea*, the LORD our God shall cut them off.

Psalm 94:17, 23

O come, let us worship and bow down: let us kneel before the LORD our maker.

For he *is* our God; and we *are* the people of his pasture, and the sheep of his hand. To day if ye will hear his voice.

Psalm 95:6, 7

Let the heavens rejoice, and let the earth be glad; let the sea roar, and the fulness thereof.

Let the field be joyful, and all that *is* therein: then shall all the trees of the wood rejoice

Before the LORD: for he cometh, for he cometh to judge the earth: he shall judge the world with righteousness, and the people with his truth.

Psalm 96:11–13

The heavens declare his righteousness, and all the people see his glory.

Psalm 97:6

Enter into his gates with thanksgiving, *and* into his courts with praise: be thankful unto him, *and* bless his name.

For the LORD *is* good; his mercy is everlasting; and his truth *endureth* to all generations.

Psalm 100:4, 5

Cause me to hear thy loveingkindness in the morning; for in thee do I trust: cause me to know the way wherein I should walk; for I lift up my soul unto thee.

Teach me to do thy will; for thou *art* my God: thy spirit *is* good; lead me into the land of uprightness.

Psalm 143:8, 10

For as the heaven is high above the earth, *so* great is his mercy toward them that fear him.

Like as a father pitieth *his* children, *so* the LORD pitieth them that fear him.

As for man, his days *are* as grass: as a flower of the field, so he flourisheth.

For the wind passeth over it, and it is gone; and the place thereof shall know it no more.

But the mercy of the LORD *is* from everlasting to everlasting upon them that fear him, and his righteousness unto children's children.

Psalm 103:11, 13, 15–17

He causeth the grass to grow for the cattle, and herb for the service of man: that he may bring forth food out of the earth;

And wine *that* maketh glad the heart of man, *and* oil to make *his* face to shine, and bread *which* strengtheneth man's heart.

The trees of the LORD are full *of sap*; the cedars of Leb'-a-non, which he hath planted:

Where the birds make their nests: *as for* the stork, the fir trees *are* her house.

The high hills *are* a refuge for the wild goats; *and* the rocks for the conies.

He appointed the moon for seasons: the sun knoweth his going down.

Thou makest darkness, and it is night: wherein all the beasts of the forest do creep *forth*.

The young lions roar after their prey, and seek their meat from God.

The sun ariseth, they gather themselves together, and lay them down in their dens.

Man goeth forth unto his work and to his labour until the evening.

O LORD, how manifold are thy works! in wisdom hast thou made them all: the earth is full of thy riches.

Psalm 104:14–24

Bless the LORD, O my soul. O LORD my God, thou art very great; though art clothed with honour and majesty.

Who coverest *thyself* with light as *with* a garment: who stretchest out the heavens like a curtain:

Who layeth the beams of his chambers in the waters: who maketh the clouds his chariot; who walketh upon the wings of the wind:

Who maketh his angels spirits; his ministers a flaming fire:

Who laid the foundations of the earth, *that* it should not be removed for ever.

Psalm 104:1–5

I understand more than the ancients, because I keep thy precepts.

I have refrained my feet from every evil way, that I might keep thy word.

I have not departed from thy judgments: for thou hast taught me.

How sweet are thy words unto my taste! *yea, sweeter* than honey to my mouth.

Psalm 119:100–103

Therefore I love thy commandments above gold; yea, above fine gold.

Psalm 119:127

Thy testimonies *are* wonderful: therefore doth my soul keep them.

Psalm 119:129

The entrance of thy words giveth light; it giveth understanding unto the simple.

Psalm 119:130

I opened my mouth, and panted: for I longed for thy commandments.

Psalm 119:131

Order my steps in thy word: and let not any iniquity have dominion over me.

Psalm 119:133

Rivers of waters run down mine eyes, because they keep not thy law.

Psalm 119:136

Thy word *is* very pure: therefore thy servant loveth it.

Psalm 119:140

I will praise thee; for I am fearfully *and* wonderfully made: marvellous *are* thy works; and *that* my soul knoweth right well.

My substance was not hid from thee, when I was made in secret, *and* curiously wrought in the lowest parts of the earth.

Thine eyes did see my substance, yet being unperfect; and in thy book all *my members* were written, *which* in continuance were fashioned, when *as yet there was* none of them.

How precious also are thy thoughts unto me, O God! How great is the sum of them!

Psalm 139:14–17